*L*oving the
World through
*J*esus

A Study of
I, II, III John and Jude

Kenn and Betty Gangel

ACCENT PUBLICATIONS
Colorado Springs, Colorado

Accent Publications
P.O. Box 36640
7125 Disc Drive
Colorado Springs, Colorado   80936

Copyright © 1994 Accent Publications
Printed in the United States of America

All rights reserved. No portion of this book may be reproduced in
any form without the written permission of the publishers, with the
exception of brief excerpts in magazine reviews.

Library of Congress catalog Card Number 94-79717

ISBN 0-89636-312-0

CONTENTS

Introduction to I, II, III John & Jude   5

1 Fellowship With the Father   7

2 Walking As Jesus Walked   13

3 Holiness and Worldliness   21

4 God's Solution for Sin   30

5 The Life of Love   37

6 Union With God   45

7 Knowledge and Faith   52

8 Blessed Assurance   59

9 A Letter of Truth   66

10 Three Church Leaders   75

11 Apostasy in the Church   83

12 Glorious Truth for Grievous Times   91

Introduction to I, II, III John & Jude

❖

*E*veryone likes to receive love letters; they are so tangible and can be enjoyed over and over again. When friends express the feelings of their hearts, it makes us love them more and want to express that love in return. John's letters give us a glimpse of his love for the Saviour and other believers. These epistles also tell how we can share that love with one another.

The First Epistle of John is always referred to as a letter despite the fact that it has no address, no reference to person or place, no direct trace of author, and no special destination. Yet the very fragrance of its pages suggests a warm, almost pastoral tone. The author appealed to his readers as though he knew their backgrounds and personal traits well.

Like the letters you and I might write, the vocabulary of I, II, and III John is simple (much like the Gospel of John). The approach is very personal; it contains no quotations or other scholarly distinctives. Experts almost unanimously attribute all three epistles to John, primarily because of its similarity with the fourth Gospel.

John's Gospel presents the way of salvation, exhorting readers to believe. His epistles display themes important to believers—life, light, and love. In John's day some distorted the message of Christ, claiming to have a superior knowledge about Him and His relationship with the Father. A few even taught that Christ never really became a man but only seemed to have human form. John's epistles emphasize the results of salvation in those who have already believed.

Jude also attacks heresy in his epistle. He writes to warn saints against apostasy and to assure them of God's ability to keep them through the most trying times. The presence of many cults and sects in our day, some of which teach the same heresies John and Jude faced, make these epistles as relevant to us now as they were for believers in the first century.

Some of the material in this book is adapted from the book *Devotions for Kindred Spirits*, published by Victor Books, Wheaton, IL: 1990.

1

"WITH YOUR HEART, BILLY, NOT YOUR EAR."

Fellowship with the Father
I JOHN 1

*J*ohn does it again! Like the wonderful fourth Gospel, this epistle shows us the reality of the Son of God. Right at the beginning John emphasizes the uniqueness of Jesus by focusing on the incarnation.

When we look at a newborn baby, we see a miracle. Created by God, sent as a gift from Him, the beginning of a new life is marvelous to observe. Spiritual birth is a miracle, too, and the Lord wants us to "see, hear, and touch" the Father in the form of His Son, Jesus Christ (I John 1:1).

Interestingly, both John and I John emphasize up front that the truths about Jesus have been verified "from the beginning."

But just as quickly, John changed the direction of thought. In his Gospel he went on to prove Jesus' deity while assuming His humanity; here he assumes Christ's deity while writing to prove His humanity.

EVIDENCES OF INCARNATION
(I John 1:1–4)

As a disciple and one of Jesus' three closest human friends, John gives an eyewitness account of the Lord's life. First, he *heard* the Lord speak of Himself and the Father. Remember how frequently John recorded Jesus' emphasis on His own words? But John also states that he *saw* the Lord with his own eyes. No one could convince him that Jesus of Nazareth was anything other than a complete human being and the Son of God.

The words *looked upon* refer to more than casual investigation. In wonder and amazement, John had walked with God's Messiah. He had *touched* the Word of life. Like a scientist, he had had the privilege of examining all of Jesus' claims in the laboratory of life. The very life of God had been manifest, and John affirmed that everything Jesus said about Himself was true.

1. (1:1) *What are the four physical ways John tells us he experienced the Word of life?*

2. (1:3) *What is the message John heard from Jesus and now declares to his readers?*

3. (1:4) *What is the purpose of this epistle?*

LIGHT FOR THE JOURNEY (I John 1:5–7)

As we get older, one of the less welcome signs of age is the increasing light necessary for everything we want to see. Whether trying to read a newspaper or struggling across a dark street at night, we seem to need more light than what is available much of the time. Christians often face that in the spiritual realities of life, too. But John promised that, in spiritual things at least, there need never be an absence, lack, or rationing of abundant light.

Light is the second of the apostle's key words in this epistle. Used throughout Scripture as a synonym for infinite holiness, purity, and righteousness, the word demonstrates here that correctness of lifestyle comes only when we walk in the light shed by God Himself. People have no excuse for natural darkness (Ephesians 5:8), willful darkness (John 3:19), or eternal darkness (Jude 13).

1. (1:5-6) *What does it mean to "walk in darkness"?*

❒ *What do we know about people who say they have fellowship with God but walk in darkness?*

2. (1:7) *What does it mean to "walk in light"?*

❏ *What is the result of walking in the light?*

3. (1:7) *What happens to the sin of those who walk in the light?*

FORGIVENESS FROM SIN (I John 1:8–10)

Verses 6, 8, and 10 in I John 1 give us three false ideas of sin, obviously common in John's day and also quite prevalent in ours. Verse 6 describes an attitude that belittles sin by disregarding its seriousness and ignoring its consequences. People who flaunt such disregard for God's standards demonstrate their lying behavior; both words and conduct show they have chosen to remain outside God's grace.

The second error is referred to in verse 8, in which John warns that only self-deceived people deny they have a sin nature. Some religious movements teach that the sin nature is removed at sanctification, and people who have progressed to that point in their spiritual walk never sin again. Mistakes maybe, and perhaps a shortcoming or two, but no real sin! Such a view directly denies the truth of verse 8.

Verse 10 deals with acts of sin rather than the nature of sin, but both effect and penalty are the same. The result of no sin nature would be no acts of sin. But John said that one who holds such an unbiblical notion makes God a liar and demonstrates that His truth has no place in his life.

1. (1:8) *About whom can it be said that they have no sin?*

2. (1:9) *What is the condition for forgiveness and cleansing?*

❏ *Why do we need forgiveness after salvation?*

❏ *How can we be cleansed from all unrighteousness?*

3. (1:10) *What is the result of saying we have not sinned?*

DIGGING DEEPER

1. *What important doctrines are taught in these verses?*

*verse 1*_____   *verse 2*_____

verse 3 _____   *verse 7*_____

verse 9 _____   *verse 10*_____

2. *Look at John 1:1,14; Philippians 2:16; Acts 5:20, and I John 1:1. What does "the Word of Life" refer to: the Lord or the message about eternal life?*

3. *How do John's words make the Christian's joy complete (1:4)?*

4. *Read again the verses about fellowship: 1:3, 1:6, 1:7. With whom are we to have fellowship and how does it actually happen?*

5. *Are there sins you need to confess (1:9)? Make a list and take them to God for cleansing. Then go to the people involved.*

❖

2

"YES, SON. I'M SURE YOU CAN WALK WITH THE LORD AND RUN WITH THE TEAM AT THE SAME TIME."

Walking As Jesus Walked
I JOHN 2: 1–11

What does God want from us? What distinctives should mark Christians as they walk before a watching world? Following their Saviour, His people pattern their lives after His.

John wanted his readers to know that their obedience is not some strange obligation God had placed on them, but rather the one they have had from the beginning. The central focus of the church emphasizes love—first to God, then to other people.

Walking is a common biblical metaphor for living. The one who claims to belong to the Lord must also adopt a lifestyle close to that modeled by the Lord Jesus.

What does that mean for us? How do the Saviour's followers "walk"? What will be different in your life this day because you know Him? What will be different because you take time to study His Word?

Gentleness, kindness, truth, grace—all these and many more qualities marked the Lord's life and therefore should be hallmarks in our lives as well. Once again, we need to be reminded that only the Holy Spirit can produce such a lifestyle in struggling, imperfect people like you and me.

HOLINESS THROUGH ADVOCACY
(I John 2:1–2)

Already we have seen two purposes of this epistle: fellowship (1:3) and joy (1:4). Now John adds a third: "These things write I unto you, that ye sin not" (2:1). We know from Romans 6:1–2 that God's abundant grace is no excuse for continued sinning; the believer is to be "dead to sin."

But since sinning is possible for believers, God has provided an Advocate who stands beside us on earth and pleads our case for mercy and forgiveness in Heaven. As the God-Man, Jesus understands the sinful weaknesses of our humanity. And He stands before Heaven's throne as the anointed Messiah, the righteous One who has no sin of His own, yet who bore our sin for us.

He became the "atoning sacrifice" (propitiation) for our sins (I John 2:2, 4:10; compare Romans 3:25). The word *propitiation* means "to cover," and the book of Hebrews details many legal aspects of how propitiation works in God's plan (Hebrews 2:17, 9:12,26). Jesus' work on the cross served the whole world, but His role as Advocate is limited to those who have accepted His offer of salvation.

1. **(2:1)** *John cites a second purpose of his epistle; what is it?*

2. **(2:1)** *What is an advocate?*

3. (2:2) *What does the word "propitiation" mean?*

☐ *What does it mean to you, in your life?*

4. (2:2) *If Jesus is the propitiation "for the sins of the whole world," will all people be saved? What does this verse mean? Check II Corinthians 5:14-15,19; Romans 3:25–26.*

OBEDIENCE TO CHRIST (I John 2:3–6)

*O*bedience serves as a test of salvation since some will claim they know the Lord even while violating His commands. Such "liars" are obviously unsaved. Notice the contrast between the Old Testament and New Testament in this passage. Moses said, "Do these things and live"; Jesus said, "Live, and because you have life, do these things." The love of God matures and increases in those who keep God's Word.

Verse 5 introduces a fourth key word in I John—*love*. And here is another test of salvation: the one who truly knows the Lord must walk, or live, as Jesus did (verse 6). Christlikeness has always been the mark of genuine disciples. God designed us to live in harmony with each other, and Jesus clearly taught that love is the hallmark—and cornerstone—of the church.

How can we do it? The indwelling Holy Spirit produces the love of Jesus in our hearts. What a joy to know that "the darkness is past" (verse 8). Though the amount of progress in one day may be difficult to measure, we can be confident that our Lord draws us closer as we keep His commandments and walk in the Light of the World.

1. (2:3,5) *How can you be sure you know Jesus and are "in him"?*

2. (2:4) *How can you spot a liar?*

3. (2:6) *What does it mean to walk as Jesus walked?*

A NEW COMMAND (I John 2:7–8)

*H*ow much do you know? Some folks think they never know enough, while others consider themselves more informed than they really are. *Know* is one of the key words in this epistle, especially when it emphasizes the knowledge Christians have of Christ. How do we know if we know Him? By how well we keep His commands (I John 2:3,5). The Greek word translated "commands" is not the common *nomos* (used 15 times by John to refer to the Mosaic Law), but a word that means "precepts" or "charges."

Jesus showed His love to people by serving them when they were in need, healing them when they were sick, talking with them when they were lonely, and crying or praying with them in their sorrow.

1. (2:7) *What commandment did they have from "the beginning"?*

❏ *What is "the beginning"?*

2. (2:8) *What is the difference between the new commandment and the old commandment?*

3. (2:8) *What "thing" is true?*

❏ *To whom does "him" refer?*

❏ *At what point in time can we say "the darkness is past, and the true light now shineth"?*

SAVED AND UNSAVED (I John 2:9-11)

Someone once wrote, "The world can be divided into two groups of people, those who divide the world into two groups of people and those who do not." This may be true, but it's not very helpful. The Bible repeatedly divides the entire human race into two groups—the saved and the unsaved.

In his Gospel, John talked about "whoever believes in Him" and "whoever does not believe." The former group will escape condemnation, but the latter group "is condemned already" (John 3:18). Bible writers never waffle on the strict line separating those who have trusted Christ and those who have not.

Now John describes these groups more thoroughly (I John 2:9–11). The unsaved person who claims to be in the light but hates his brother, walks in darkness, loses his way, and causes others to stumble.

In Mammoth Cave, electric lights have been installed so visitors can see its beauty. But when the lights are turned off, people experience total darkness, a darkness that can almost be felt, a darkness that leaves them feeling totally helpless. Spiritual darkness brings that kind of helplessness too.

1. (2:9) *Why would hating other Christians prove that a person is not a believer?*

❏ *What kind of actions or attitudes would result from such hatred? Church fights? Grudges? Gossip?*

2. (2:10) *What does it mean to say that there is "none occasion of stumbling" in somebody who loves other Christians?*

3. (2:11) *What is the darkness that blinds people who hate others?*

DIGGING DEEPER

1. *Using a Bible dictionary, look up the words "know," "knowledge," "light," "darkness," and "blinded." How does the fellowship with God mentioned in chapter 1, affect the knowledge of God discussed in chapter 2?*

2. *Make a list of as many of God's commands as you can think of or find in the Bible. Now do a self-check on how well you are obeying those commands (2:3). Do you truly know Him?*

Commands   How well do I obey?

3. *A more complete picture of abiding in Christ can be found in John 15:1–14. Read this passage and make a list of what will happen in your life "if" you abide in the vine.*

4. *Do you have hate in your heart toward a Christian brother or sister? Write out your prayer of confession and repentance. Then go and make things right with your fellow believer.*

"I'LL BET IT'LL BE EVEN HARDER THAN USUAL TO AVOID THE ATTRACTION OF THE WORLD HERE."

Holiness and Worldliness
I JOHN 2:12–29

A friend tells the story of a flight from Boston to Dallas in the summer of 1987 which departed six hours late. Tired Friday-afternoon businessmen were angry about the problem. The man across the aisle growled at the flight attendant every time she walked by. Since approaching him seemed a hopeless idea, our friend walked back to the galley to commend the flight attendant on her self-control and the way she handled the situation. He asked her name, suggesting he wanted to write American Airlines and express appreciation. She responded, "I don't work for this airline; I work for Jesus Christ."

First John 2:15–17 may represent the most important

teaching in the Bible on the subject of worldliness. We often describe worldliness according to a list of "don'ts" which Christians should avoid. To be sure, serious Christians do avoid behaviors condemned in Scripture, but John makes it clear that worldliness is primarily an attitude.

Loving the world is not some accidental mistake God's people might fall into on occasion; rather, it is a definite love relationship. John uses one of his favorite words here, *agape*, the strongest Greek term for love and the same word used of God's love in John 3:16. Sinful cravings (illegitimate desires), the lust of the eyes (sensory desires), and boastful speech (self-pride) all stem from our sinful natures and are at cross-purposes with our loving God.

Loving the world is futile, said John, because it is "being caused to pass away" while those who obey the Father will live forever.

Loving the world displays a character inconsistent with the nature of God. Christians must show the world that they belong to a different kingdom and, by God's grace, can walk above the lure and attraction of worldliness.

PERSONAL APPEALS (I John 2:12–14)

*J*ohn switches his focus to three classes of people, people measured not by their relationship to the Lord but by their level of spiritual maturity (I John 2:12–14). Every church, regardless of size, includes these three kinds of people. And God's Spirit wrote through His apostle to speak to congregations in every century, including ours.

First, John addresses the "little children" because their sins have been forgiven "for his name's sake." These people are young in the faith. The metaphor of children emphasizes the biblical doctrine of adoption. And John uses titles that speak both of kinship (*teknia*) and subordination (*paidia*).

Next John turns to the "fathers," because they know him "that is from the beginning" (verse 13). These are mature believers. Lest anyone think John limited this passage to men, though, the word translated "fathers" here could be rendered "parents" and appears just that way in Hebrews 11:23. Like Paul's injunction to older Christians in Titus 2:1–3, John expected the lives of mature believers to reflect their years of walking with the Lord.

Then the passage speaks to energetic young believers (verse 13) in the process of growing up in Christ. These growing Christians have overcome the wicked one and are maturing spiritually. The growth pattern of the family and of the vine is seen: New converts become growing Christians who turn into mature saints.

1. **(2:12)** *Why are believers' sins forgiven?*

2. **(2:13)** *Name the three groups of this verse and the reasons why John writes them.*

3. **(2:14)** *Why mention the fathers and the young men a second time?*

PERSONAL ATTRACTIONS (I John 2:15–17)

Worldliness is much more an attitude than an action, and it is the opposite of worship. These three verses may represent the most important section of Scripture on the subject of worldliness as John tries to show us how genuinely attractive the world can be and what we should do about that.

1. (2:15) *Name some of the things that are in the world and why you might love them.*

☐ *Why would loving the world keep you from loving the Father?*

2. (2:16) *Give some examples of the three categories John lists.*

• *Lust of the flesh*

• *Lust of the eyes*

• *Pride of life*

❏ *What does it mean that these are "of the world," not the Father?*

3. (2:17) *What happens to the one who does the will of God?*

❏ *How do you know or determine God's will for your life?*

PERSONAL APOSTASY (I John 2:18–25)

Absolute truth seems hard to find in these days of glass diamonds, simulated pearls, and instant foods. Even Christians develop fake relationships because we want others to think well of us. But only the Holy Spirit can produce true knowledge and help us live out God's absolute truth.

Virtually every New Testament writer viewed the days in which he lived as the "end times" or the "last hour." Teaching about the antichrist was common, so John warned that many who represent his spirit and ideals were already in the world (I John 2:18–27). Certainly their number has increased dramatically since John wrote these words.

Verse 19 helps us understand why some people who profess Christ leave the faith and go "out from us." They are apostate because they never had a life-changing experience with the Saviour. They were "faking it." Now, as they reject the Gospel, they merely show their true colors. Their very departure marks them as never having been a true part of Christ's body.

1. (2:18) *Why would John use the phrase "little children" here?*

❏ *What does John mean by "many antichrists"?*

2. (2:19) *Restate this verse in your own words.*

❏ *Think about the church today. How would we recognize "antichrists" within it?*

3. (2:22–23) *What does it mean to deny that Jesus is the Christ, the Son of God?*

4. (2:24-25) *What great promise do you have?*

☐ *How can the Word of God "abide" or "remain" in us?*

PERSONAL ANOINTING (I John 2:26–29)

*T*rue believers listen to the Holy Spirit and therefore know the truth. Only "liars" deny that Jesus is the Messiah come in the flesh. They reject Christ's incarnation and deity. Just as apostasy marks phony Christians, we identify true believers by their abiding and their anointing. Surely this "anointing" links back to verse 20 and refers to the Holy Spirit who lives in the born-again person.

No human teacher is the *ultimate* source of a believer's instruction. The inner witness of God's Spirit leads us in His truth.

1. (2:26) *Who was being seduced and who are the seducers referred to in this verse?*

2. (2:27) *What is the "anointing"?*

3. (2:28) *Why does John use the phrase "little children" again here?*

❐ *What would make us ashamed before Jesus when He returns?*

4. (2:29) *Why is Jesus righteous?*

❐ *Why does "doing righteousness" show others that you are born again in Jesus?*

DIGGING DEEPER

1. *What should our churches do to teach Christians about worldliness without being legalistic?*

2. *Name some characteristics of false prophets or antichrists.*

❏ *Think of some false prophets. How did they obtain followers and what eventually happened to them? What are some ways we can avoid being tricked by them?*

3. *Is it possible to believe in God the Father but deny Jesus the Son? How could you use I John 2:23–24 to support your position?*

4. *When people watch your life, do they know you are abiding in Christ? What do they see in you to give evidence of new life (2:28–29)?*

❖

"WELL YES, SON. THAT'S ONE REASON YOU SHOULDN'T PRACTICE SIN."

God's Solution for Sin
I JOHN 3:1–10

*T*he headline in our local paper blared, "Two Killed, One Hurt in Church Shooting." Apparently when four deacons got into an argument, one pulled a gun and started shooting. Because sin found a place in the heart of a church leader, the entire church suffered the consequences.

According to John, habitual sinning stands contrary to the behavior of a genuine Christian. We see the emphasis on habit in almost every verb in I John 3:4–10; most are in the present tense. Sin is lawlessness, John writes, and Christ came to fulfill the law. He removes sinful lifestyles from those who turn to Him.

Once again, John measured hearts by what he could see in people's conduct. Someone who continually practices sinning demonstrates that he has never known the Lord experientially. He may know much about the Bible and the gospel, but if the living Christ indwells him through the Holy Spirit, a pattern of perpetual sinning cannot occur.

In the opposite corner stands the habitual sinner, unable to shake such behavior because it demonstrates his connection to Satan (verse 10). Practicing righteousness reveals the new birth; practicing sin reveals a lost condition apart from God.

THE HOPE OF GOD'S CHILDREN (I John 3:1–3)

*H*ow can Christians make right choices between worldliness and holiness? The certainty that Jesus is coming again should motivate us to choose and live out righteous behavior. If we really believe that the Lord could return at any time, we will behave in ways that would please Him (I John 2:28—3:3). This includes living so that we will have "confidence and not be ashamed before Him" (2:28), having done what is right (verse 29), and leading pure lives (3:3).

1. **(3:1)** *Why does the world not "know" Christians?*

❐ *How would you define, explain, or illustrate the love the Father has given to you?*

2. **(3:2)** *What will it be like when Jesus comes?*

3. (3:3) *What is the practical value of expecting Christ's return?*

THE LIFE OF GOD'S CHILDREN
(I John 3:4–6)

*J*ohn expresses amazement at the kind of love it took for us to become the children of God. Unsaved people cannot understand the reality of the new birth; they do not know Christ personally. But those born of God, who live in His likeness, understand the spiritual nature. Through sanctification they become more like the Lord as they wait for His return.

These verses describe the horrible error of mistaking a false spiritual life for reality. The first three verbs of verse 6 are all present tense, indicating ongoing activity.

1. (3:4) *What is sin?*

❐ *What is law?*

❐ *How are they related?*

2. (3:5) *Why did Jesus become human?*

3. (3:6) *Do Christians who try to live righteously really "sin not"? What does this mean?*

☐ *What do we know about people who habitually sin?*

THE LOVE OF GOD'S CHILDREN
(I John 3:7–10)

Among believers, love provides a test of life. John must have paid attention to the Lord's words in the Upper Room the night before the crucifixion. There Jesus taught His disciples that the world would measure the reality of their relationship to Him by the way they related to each other (John 13:35).

1. (3:7) *What is righteousness?*

☐ *Give examples of righteous living in your life. Why are they righteous?*

❏ *Restate this verse in your own words.*

2. (3:8) *Here we find another reason for Jesus' life on earth. What is it?*

3. (3:9) *Why don't those who are born again live a sinful lifestyle or sin on a regular basis?*

4. (3:10) *How do the children of God differ from the children of the devil?*

DIGGING DEEPER

1. *In what ways will Christians be like Jesus (3:2)?*

❐   *When will this transformation take place?*

2. *In the first 10 verses of chapter 3, John takes a serious view of sin. Make a list of the consequences of sin given in these verses.*

3. *Make another list of the qualities which God expects to see in our lives as a result of His righteousness in us.*

4. *How would you define "righteousness" as John uses it in verses 7 and 10?*

5. *What is God's solution for sin:*

    • for the world?

    • in the believer?

❖

"I CAN SEE THAT YOUR HEART IS RIGHT. NOW LET'S FIND OUT IF IT'S HEALTHY."

The Life of Love
I JOHN 3:11–24

A mass of small water droplets or tiny ice crystals floating in the air, clouds can reflect the beauty of a sunset, bring refreshing rain, envelop with the silence of fog, or cover the earth with a blanket of snow. Like a cloud, a conscience filled and controlled by Christ's love creates beauty, refreshment, and peace in the Christian's life.

This passage, like John 13, reminds us that love reflects the status of our hearts. Furthermore, love for Christ att acts hatred from the world. It may not be expressed in words, but the Bible repeatedly reminds us that the things of Satan and the things of Christ cannot peacefully co-exist.

LOVE AS A TEST OF LIFE (I John 3:11–15)

*T*he central theme of I John 2 now appears in I John 3. Cain represents the epitome of what happens when sin confronts righteousness. Cain hated Abel because they had different natures. In the same way, the world hates believers, sometimes even to the point of death. Anyone who habitually hates others contains within himself the characteristics of a murderer (Matthew 5:21–22).

Hardly a day goes by that we do not see evidence of Satan's fingerprints in the world around us. Murder, corruption, cruelty—such behaviors reflect the difference between hate and love and should draw Christians to a passage like this which describes "the life of love" the Holy Spirit wants to produce in us.

1. **(3:12)** *Why did Cain kill his brother? (See Genesis 4:8-24.)*

2. **(3:14)** *How can we know that we have passed from death to life?*

❑ *What actions would give evidence of this in a believer's life?*

❑ *What does "brother" in this verse mean? Does it refer only to Christians? If so, how could a believer abide in death?*

3. (3:15) *What does this passage say about a murderer?*

SACRIFICE AS A TEST OF LIFE
(I John 3:16–20)

What good is a conscience? Usually conscience operates according to law or social codes of morality, but most people would probably argue that Christians should have the most highly developed, most sensitive consciences of anyone in the world. First John 3:19–24 and other passages remind us that the role of the conscience in the believer is augmented by the Holy Spirit's ministry within us.

1. (3:16) *How do we know God loves us?*

2. (3:17) *What point is John trying to make by this question?*

3. (3:18) *Name some ways we can love in deed and in truth.*

☐ *Why are words alone worthless?*

4. (3:20) *What does this verse mean to you?*

FAITH AS A TEST OF LIFE (I John 3:21–24)

*J*ust as the Holy Spirit assures us of proper decisions and behavior, He relieves us of guilt and uneasiness. When He convicts, however, we are turned to the Lord for forgiveness and cleansing. All this relates closely to our prayer lives. If we keep our lives clean at the Spirit's prompting, and keep His commandments, we can ask for those things that are within His will and expect to have them.

Consider the importance of the Holy Spirit's residence in your life. More than just a test of salvation, His presence is your key to godliness and contentment here on earth. Learn more about this great truth and practice the awareness of your resident Friend (Romans 8:16; Galatians 3:14; Ephesians 4:30).

1. (3:22) *What does this prayer promise mean to you? Can we take it literally?*

2. (3:23) *Why does John use the word "commandment" so frequently?*

❏ *What difference, if any, does John intend between the two commandments he mentions?*

❏ *How does this verse relate to Luke 10:27 and Matthew 22:37-39?*

3. (3:24) *How do we know that Jesus abides in us?*

DIGGING DEEPER

1. *What are some practical ways church members can demonstrate love to each other?*

❑ *How can individual Christians demonstrate love to the community in general?*

❑ *What will you do this month do demonstrate Christ's love to your community?*

2. Do a parallel study of John 3:16 and I John 3:16. What do you see in each verse? What truths stand out?

3. This two-fold command to believe in Christ and to love one another appears often in Christ's teachings. Read John 3:18 and John 13:34. What other passages clearly teach these two aspects of Christian living? Why would it be repeated so often?

4. What is the ministry of the Holy Spirit? Read John 16:7–15. Write down some of the things Jesus said the Holy Spirit would do for believers.

5. What did John mean by saying that people who hate others are murderers? Isn't it possible for Christians to actually "hate" other Christians at some time, for some good reason? Discuss your answer in detail.

6. List some ways Christians can lay down their lives for other Christians. What specific things do we do that could be described in such strong terminology?

7. This passage seems to make a close connection between a clear conscience and answers to prayer (see verses 21 and 22). Name some conscience-damaging thoughts or behaviors that would hinder your prayer life.

"MOM, MEET JIMMY. HE'S A FRIEND OF A FRIEND."

Union With God
I JOHN 4

A counselor was out with his group of young campers one dark night. With only a flashlight to guide them, the boys were frightened by the darkness and wanted to turn back. The counselor assured them that even though the light would shine only a short distance in front of them, it was enough to lead them back to the camp one step at a time. Jesus, our Light, guides us through life with His love and truth one step at a time. When we wander from Him, He loves us and draws us back again.

We come now to an important doctrinal section of I John. The apostle wanted to be sure his readers understood that love must be grounded in truth, so he encouraged them to be discerning about what they believed, especially regarding spiritual things (I John 4:1–6). Belief in the incarnation becomes the demarcation line between truth and error.

Though the spirit of the antichrist already permeates the world, believers overcome that force through the indwelling power of the Holy Spirit. The teaching of false teachers, whether in John's day or ours, finds its basis in this world's systems. All false cults and heresies originate in the mind of natural, fallen man who is controlled by a sin nature dominated by Satan. The truth of Christianity comes from God through revelation and faith.

Christians need have no fear of the world now or the judgment of the future. As patient foster parents slowly change an abused and frightened child into a trusting family member, so the Father's love for us can make us productive and confident members of the household of faith.

Our relationship with God is the foundation for our relationship with other people. We first experience His love for us; then we reflect that love, demonstrating the love of the Father to His other children as well as those not in the family.

TRY THE SPIRITS (I John 4:1–6)

*B*ecause the spirit of evil and error permeates the world, Christians must always be on guard. So what can we expect? Opposition and strife. When we proclaim God's truth from His Word, we should anticipate that many will reject it and scorn the messenger. We must measure results by our relationship to the pure truth of the gospel, not by some interpretation we happen to treasure. God holds us responsible for sharing the message; responses remain in His hands.

1. (4:1) *How can we "try the spirits"? What "spirits" are we testing?*

2. (4:2–3) *What is the key test to determine which spirits are of God and which are not?*

3. (4:4) *How do Christians overcome evil opposition?*

4. (4:6) *How do we know the difference between the spirit of truth and the spirit of error?*

LOVE OTHER CHRISTIANS (I John 4:7-16)

*H*ow do Christians best reflect the nature of God in them? Through church attendance? Through correct doctrine? By giving to missions? As important as all three may be for all of us, none is the correct answer. John said that we best show what God is like when we love other people (I John 4:7–17). Yet we only know how to love because we have known and seen God's love in action—namely, that He loves us and sent His Son as an atoning sacrifice for our sins (verse 10).

Verse 10 is the key to this section. The substitution Christ made for us—His death instead of ours, His life sacrificed to cover our sin—stands as the ultimate demonstration of love. Love as a habit of life comes to us modeled by the Father and the Son. For emphasis, John repeats much of what he has already told us in this letter.

1. (4:7-16) *Count the number of times some form of the word "love" appears in these verses.*

2. (4:8) *What do we know about people who don't love other people?*

3. (4:10) *What does it mean that Jesus is the propitiation for our sins?*

❐ *If you have not already done so, memorize this verse.*

4. (4:12) *If we love each other, what does that let others see?*

5. (4:13) *What is the Holy Spirit's role in Christian love?*

PUT ASIDE YOUR FEARS (I John 4:17–21)

*T*his section closes by contrasting love with fear. Fear has to do with judgment, but love recognizes that Christ already took our punishment. Fear shows no confidence about eternity, but love reflects on our union with God through the Saviour.

The role of love in the Christian life has been called "the explosive power of a new affection." Rather than demanding that His children give up their worldly "toys" and desires, our Lord places within us an overwhelming love and His desires, making us willing to put Him first.

Even fear, so common to many people in this world, must succumb to the power of His love (I John 4:18–21).

Verse 19 says, "We love him because He first loved us." This statements is true, of course, but the context in this passage also emphasizes love for other people, made possible by the impulsive and explosive power of a new affection.

1. (4:17) *What does it mean to "have boldness in the day of judgment"?*

❐ *What is the "day of judgment" for a Christian?*

2. (4:18) *In what ways does love free us from fear?*

❐ *What does this verse mean in relation to the fears of life we all face or does it relate only to spiritual fears?*

3. (4:19) *Why do you love Jesus?*

4. (4:21) *Why does John constantly repeat the admonition to love each other? Why is it so important?*

DIGGING DEEPER

1. *Love is a key word and theme in this chapter. Go through your Bible and find references to God, Jesus, or the Holy Spirit. What is the link between the triune God and loving behavior?*

2. *According to verse 19, what is the ultimate expression of love?*

3. What specific things do verses 15-17 and 21 say believers will do as part of God's family?

❏ How are you expressing these things?

❖

7

"I AM DOING MY SUNDAY SCHOOL LESSON. JESUS IS ON THE HISTORY CHANNEL."

Knowledge and Faith
I JOHN 5:1–12

"Seeing is believing," we say in our culture, and at least one state's motto (Missouri) is nationally known as a "show me" or "prove it" attitude. But John's books turn that motto around and remind us, "Believing is seeing." The particular target of faith here, as elsewhere in this epistle, is the incarnation (I John 5:1–5). What marks those who truly belong to the Saviour? They believe that Jesus is the virgin-born Son of God who came in human flesh. In short, He is the Messiah.

Furthermore, whoever loves the Father will also love His children (4:20). And how do we implement this love? By keeping His commandments.

The hymn, "Faith is the Victory," comes directly from these verses. In the original text, the word translated "victory" and "overcome" is the same, appearing in noun form only here in the entire New Testament. We gain victory over the world, John claims, because we participate in the overcoming power of Jesus Christ, the Son of God.

Medical missionary Bill Barnett was sent by God to an island off Mozambique, where it is illegal to witness overtly. Authorities, however, allowed him to practice medicine and to answer questions. To keep the spirit as well as the letter of the law, he refused to discuss Christianity with anyone unless that person asked him three times, which happened with some frequency during the years of his ministry there. His life was a threefold witness!

Cerinthus, a popular heretic living during John's day, taught that the person of God "came on" Jesus the man at the time of His baptism and then left Him just before the cross. But John allows no such confusion of the gospel; the Jesus who was baptized was the same Lord who died for our sins on the cross.

How do we know this? How did these early Christians to whom John wrote this letter grasp and hold on to this and other truths? Because the Spirit testifies of such things and the Spirit is truth. Three facts witness to the truth: the presence of the Holy Spirit; the historical record of Jesus' baptism, and His death on the cross for us. The reality of these historical witnesses remains foundational to our faith. Our belief is grounded in accurate historical record.

EXPERIENCING GOD'S VICTORY
(I John 5:1–5)

John discovers the purpose of life in love, obedience, and faith. He emphasizes the great victory we have as children of God. Sometimes, however, that victory does not seem very realistic. We get discouraged and even defeated by our own failures and the obstacles to faith all around us. When we are least sure of God's presence, we most need to accept it by faith and act on it.

1. (5:1) *Who is the one "that begat" and who is the one "that is begotten of him"?*

☐ *What is the sole basis of salvation?*

☐ *If you believe that, what does it include? What does that mean?*

2. (5:2) *How do we know that we love the children of God?*

3. (5:3) *Write several synonyms for "grievous." One is "burdensome." Use them to complete the sentence, "The commandments of God are not...."*

4. (5:4) *In what practical ways does faith overcome the world?*

ACCEPTING GOD'S TESTIMONY
(I John 5:6–9)

*T*hink how many people know about the baptism and death of Jesus—even about His resurrection—and yet have chosen to reject the truth and meaning of those events. No one becomes a believer and no believer grows in faith without yielding to the Holy Spirit's efforts to proclaim and explain truth.

1. (5:6) *What does it mean to say that Jesus came "by water and blood"?*

2. (5:7) *Who are the three that bear record in Heaven?*

3. (5:8) *Name the three who bear witness on earth.*

4. (5:9) *What is the basic truth John is trying to make in this verse?*

TRUSTING GOD'S SON (I John 5:10–12)

As in I John 5:6–9, so in verses 10–13 "testimony" is a key word. John warned that rejecting the Spirit's testimony about the gospel leads to lying and death. And what precisely is that testimony? "God hath given to us eternal life, and this life is in his Son. He that hath the Son hath life; and he that hath not the Son of God hath not life" (verses 11–12).

These verses contain the gospel "in a nutshell." Like the Gospel of John, this epistle centers in the Person and work of the Saviour. But John's Gospel was written to unbelievers to call them to faith in Christ; I John was written to call them to assurance (verse 13).

1. (5:10) *What does it mean to have "the witness" in yourself?*

❐ *How does one make God a liar?*

2. (5:11–12) *Who has life and who doesn't?*

❐ *If you have not previously memorized these verses, now would be a good time to do so.*

DIGGING DEEPER

1. *Through the Holy Spirit, Christians can overcome the world. But what happens when we don't? What causes temporary defeats and how can we recapture that victory?*

2. *Love fills the words of this book and this passage. Name three practical, realistic ways you show love to other believers.*

1)

2)

3)

3. *Some marginal notes indicate that verse 7 has no manuscript evidence. That it was probably not in the original Greek text. How do you handle challenges like that?*

4. *Count the number of times the word "witness" appears in this passage. Who are these witnesses? What do they do?*

5. *Describe "eternal life" without using either word in your description (verse 11).*

6. *What does verse 12 mean after death?*

❖

8

"THANK GOODNESS FOR YOUR TWENTY-FOUR HOUR HOTLINE!"

Blessed Assurance
I JOHN 5:13–21

*K*nowing God intimately will see us through the hard times. When we understand we are His children, that He has given us His truth, all else may crumble around us but we rely on the known God.

Certain knowledge stands as one of John's central goals in this epistle. Three of the last four verses in I John 5 begin with the words, "we know." What is this information of which the early Christians were so confident?

1. True Christians come only from God.
2. The whole world lies in Satan's control.
3. God's Son has come and explained the Father to us.

One valuable result of certain knowledge is prayer. If we know Christ, and know that God hears us when we pray, a Christian praying in God's will is like a sailboat carried along by the force of the winds. Direction and mobility come when we adjust ourselves to the flow of His plans and timing.

Interesting, isn't it, that John links our prayer for fellow Christians with the confidence of answered prayer (verses 14–15). So often we pray for *our*selves, *our* needs, *our* wants, *our* hurts and *our* struggles. That's fine, of course, but John reminds us to remember others as well.

Why not make your prayer time this month a special emphasis for brothers and sisters in Christ who may be involved in some sin known to you. Ask the Lord to keep them alive, to bring them to confession and cleansing, and to make them productive in His service once again.

CONFIDENCE THROUGH PRAYER
(I John 5:13–15)

*P*erhaps more than any other Bible writer John talks about praying "in the name of Jesus." Those exact words do not appear, but he certainly implies that prayer is absolutely linked to our relationship with the Saviour and confidence in prayer depends upon praying for things that please Him.

1. (5:13) *What two results does John want his book to have in the lives of his readers?*

2. (5:14) *What does it mean to ask "according to his will"?*

3. (5:14) *How can we know God's will?*

4. (5:15) *How can you be certain God hears you when you pray?*

COMMISSION OF SIN (I John 5:16–17)

*D*o you know of anyone who has sinned a "sin that leads to death"? First John 5:14–18 is a difficult passage, a passage on which scholars have different opinions. Notice that the sinner is a "brother," obviously a fellow Christian. Furthermore, God expects the praying friend to know whether the sin in question is "unto death" or not.

Some believe the sin leading to death is a denial of the incarnation, since John emphasized that doctrine so strongly throughout this letter. Others prefer an interpretation that centers on physical death, perhaps from the punishment of God as in the case of Ananias and Sapphira. We see John saying, "If you see another Christian sinning, pray that God will keep him alive if he has not sinned seriously enough to warrant death. But remember, not all sin results in death."

1. (5:16) *What is "a sin unto death"?*

❑ *How can we know if a person for whom we might pray has committed the sin unto death?*

2. (5:17) *How does the sin unto death differ from a sin not unto death?*

3. (5:16-17) *Why do you think John introduces this aspect of prayer at this point in his letter?*

CAUTION AGAINST IDOLATRY
(I John 5:18–21)

*T*he stern and final warning against idolatry (verse 21) suggests rather firmly that any concept of God apart from Jesus Christ is idolatry. In John's view, all agnostics, cultists, and others who deny the incarnation and related truths of Christ's ministry should be labeled "idolaters."

How essential for us to recognize that idolatry can exist in the mind! We dare not limit it to images or carved religious objects. Even Christians, when they substitute some personal or cultural idea for the true biblical teaching about God, engage in a form of idolatry. Do you follow only those worship patterns which you see in His Word?

1. (5:18) *What does John mean when he says those who are born again do not sin?*

2. (5:19) *Name some ways that "the whole world lieth in wickedness."*

3. (5:20) *What understanding did Jesus give us when He came?*

☐ *Why would it be important for John to emphasize that God is true?*

4. (5:21) *Why would John end his letter with this warning?*

DIGGING DEEPER

1. *Identify the major doctrine verse 13 teaches. What other New Testament passages treat this subject?*

2. (5:14–15) *This is surely a key passage on prayer. Find two or three other such passages in the New Testament. What do they mean to your prayer life?*

3. (5:16–17) *How would you put these verses into practice in your congregation? Should it be done only by a pastor, elder or deacon?*

4. *"We know" are key words in the passage. Make a list of the things verses 5:13,15,18,19,20 tell us "we know."*

5. *Literal, physical forms of idolatry were common in Old Testament days, but what about today? What are some modern, North American idols?*

❑ *What is John telling believers today?*

9

"THIS IS A BOOK ABOUT TRUTH AND LOVE. YOU NEED TO PAY PARTICULAR ATTENTION TO THE TRUTH PART."

A Letter of Truth
II JOHN

Ron Hembree, in his book *Good Morning, Lord*, told this story.

One day several young boys went hunting crabs, placing the ugly creatures in a wicker basket after they were caught. Several adults passing by on the beach noticed that the basket had no lid. One of them called to the boys, "Hey, you kids had better cover that basket or the crabs will get away."

"No they won't," replied the lad. "If one crab tries to climb up, the others pull him down."

Too often, we see this behavior exhibited among Christians. We see it as we relate to and exemplify Jesus to unbelievers. It's especially true in the workplace where it often seems that our faith has no part in such affairs. And it is the exact opposite of what John tells us should happen among believers whose task it is to help each other up and model Christ.

This book talks about the importance of combining truth and love in our attitudes and behavior. John emphasizes that some people care for neither. These "deceivers" have abandoned the teaching about the Father and the Son; they go beyond the limits of pure doctrine and deliberately confuse and lead astray those who listen to them.

Lying seems to come easily to all of us. It begins when we are young children, quickly denying wrongdoing in order to keep from being punished. As adults we sometimes avoid telling the whole truth in order to advance our own cause or perhaps to save money. In II John 1–6, John takes aim at the importance of truth, reminding us that Jesus came to earth in truth and love.

THE TRUTH DEMONSTRATED (II John 1-6)

Whether "the elect lady" (verse 1) represents a local church or a real person, the central theme of this tiny epistle stands clear—truth. After a loving and doctrinal introduction, the apostle suggests three ways in which God's truth is demonstrated.

The first is the Father's own Word establishing truth through His commands. The Father's truth has also been shown firsthand through His Son who has revealed grace, mercy, and peace—qualities which mark not only the life of our Lord but should also be evident in the lives of those who say they are "Christ"-ians.

God's truth is also reflected by a group John called "some of your children." Was he referring to a remnant of the congregation, other Christians led to the Lord by this person, or the young people of the church? Commentators vary in their views, but one thing is clear: the Bible commends all who live their faith by walking in the truth.

Third, we see truth in the love of the saints. What is more important in a group of believers—truth or love?

John argues that these two absolutely essential ingredients must be seen in tandem. Just as Jesus came "full of grace and truth" (John 1:14), His people are expected to speak the truth in love, never compromising one for the sake of the other.

1. **(verse 1)** *To whom do you think the "elect lady" refers?*

2. **(verse 2)** *In what way will the truth be with us forever?*

3. **(verse 3)** *List the five gifts from God found in this verse.*

4. **(verse 4)** *To whom does the word "children" in this verse refer?*

   ❑ *What does it mean to walk in truth?*

5. (verse 5) *What is the commandment that we have had "from the beginning"?*

❑ *Why do you think John is reminding his reader of this commandment?*

6. (verse 6) *How do we show love for God?*

❑ *What does that mean in your life? How do you show love for God?*

THE TRUTH VIOLATED (II John 7-13)

*H*ow should sincere Christians react to false teachers? John issues two practical warnings: watch out so you don't lose your full reward, and don't welcome such people or assist them in any way. Apparently, John's immediate readers were already doing this, since his wording that suggests they should stop their behavior.

Like many of us, John felt that touchy matters of doctrine were best dealt with in person, so he deferred further discussion until he could see his friends. At that visit he intended to accomplish more than just theological correction; he wanted them to experience real joy from their collective fellowship. What a grand picture of the body of Christ—demonstrating truth, avoiding violators of truth, and sharing loving joy with one another.

1. **(verse 7)** *Why does John call deceivers "antichrists"?*

   ❑ *What deception are they trying to accomplish?*

2. **(verse 8)** *What is "a full reward"?*

   ❑ *What things might we lose?*

3. **(verse 9)** *Restate this verse in your own words.*

   ❑ *What is the doctrine of Christ?*

4. (verses 10-11) *What does John refer to by the words "this doctrine"?*

❐ *In a modern application of these verses, whom might you turn away from your door? Does this seem harsh? Why wouldn't John say to witness to them or bring them in and talk with them?*

❐ *What does it mean to bid someone "God speed"?*

❐ *Why are the "deeds" or work of these people evil? (You may also want to look at John 3:18-20.)*

5. (verse 12) *How could John deliver his message more clearly "face to face"?*

❐ *Why would that make their joy "full"?*

6. (verse 13) *To whom does John refer in this last verse of the letter?*

7. (verse 13) *Since this is a letter, not a prayer, why would John end with the word "Amen"?*

DIGGING DEEPER

1. *Think again about the possible meanings of "elect lady," "children," and "elect sister." Now that you have studied the whole epistle, what's your opinion on who they represent?*

2. *"Truth" is surely a major theme in this letter. As you think about your church, what are several key elements in the "truth" you believe?*

3. *What can Christian parents do to help their children not only believe truth but walk in it (verse 4)?*

4. *How do you feel about obeying a passage like verses 7-11 that tells you not to be hospitable to some people?*

5. *Perhaps John is warning his readers against cultic teaching. What central factor would identify a cult?*

❑ *What cults are prominent in your area?*

❑ *How can your congregation reach them with the truth?*

6. One way of studying a Bible chapter is to find and state the central idea in one sentence. In your view, what is the central idea of II John?

7. John's words about writing remind us that we may "owe" a letter or two. Who could you help spiritually by sending an encouraging note? Why would this help them?

<u>Who</u>   <u>Why</u>

Now do it.

10

Three Church Leaders
III JOHN

Shirley has the gift of hospitality. Her home is always open to friends, travelers, and even strangers. The weekly Bible study meets in her home even when Shirley is out of town since several friends have keys to her house. Everyone knows her attitude: "Just make yourself at home." People who need a place to stay often bunk in at Shirley's for months at a time. She provides a good example of John's admonition in III John 1–8.

The only third epistle in the Bible urges believers to enjoy and exercise fellowship with those who walk in truth. Four times John refers to Gaius as "beloved," commending him for his hospitality to other Christians. And look again at verse 2; what condition would you be in if your physical health were as good or as poor as your spiritual health?

When a young man died of cancer in 1977, the memorial card for the funeral quoted these words by John Henry Newman:

> *God has created me to render Him some definite service. He has committed some work to me which He has not committed to another. I have a mission. I may never know it in this life but I shall be told it in the next. Therefore, I will trust Him. Whatever I am, I can never be thrown away. If I am in sickness, my sickness may serve Him. If I am in sorrow, my sorrow may serve Him. He does nothing in vain. He knows what He is about.*

When Dwight Eisenhower was a general, he used to demonstrate the art of leadership with a simple piece of string. Putting it on a table he'd say, "Pull it and it will follow wherever you wish; push it and it will go nowhere at all. It's just that way when it comes to leading people." The church needs leaders today—leaders who can "pull" by loving and caring, leaders like Demetrius and Gaius.

FAITHFUL GAIUS (III John 1-8)

*G*aius ministered through hospitality to itinerant preachers who were strangers to him. Their reports came back to John in Ephesus, creating a positive reputation for Gaius as one who put his love into practice. Because people like Gaius cared for the travel needs of these servants, the gospel could be proclaimed freely to the heathen. And those who offered them hospitality shared in the evangelism.

Some say hospitality is a dead art among believers today. Yet the New Testament consistently urges us to show such care for others, even strangers. Let's take passages like this seriously and "revive" hospitality among God's people in our day with whatever resources God has given you. Let it begin with you and your family.

1. **(verses 1-4)** *Why does John refer to himself as "the elder"?*

☐ *What does his wish in verse 2 say about Gaius?*

☐ *Why is John so excited about Gaius' faithfulness to the truth?*

2. **(verse 5)** *Who is John referring to when he uses the words "brethren" and "strangers"?*

3. **(verses 6–7)** *What does the word charity mean here?*

☐ *Why and how is it linked to his hospitality?*

☐ *Do you think Paul's letter to the Romans (12:9-13) may have influenced Gaius? Why?*

❏ *To whom does John refer when he commends Gaius's hospitality?*

"Before the church" —

Those whom he brings "forward on their journey" —

"For his name's sake" —

"The Gentiles" —

4. (verse 8) *In what ways are people who show hospitality "fellowhelpers to the truth"?*

ARROGANT DIOTREPHES (III John 9-11)

Diotrephes represents precisely the opposite of what we have learned about Gaius. He rejected John's earlier letter recommending hospitality and insisted that other people in the church behave just as he did.

What kind of fellow must he have been? Obviously very arrogant and demanding. Perhaps he held some office and tried to control the congregation. John clearly condemned that kind of autocratic leadership.

1. (verse 9) *Why would John have written his admonition to the church rather than to Diotrephes directly?*

❒ *In what ways do church leaders take inappropriate preeminence?*

2. (verse 10) *Think about the kind of situation that might have been going on in this first-century church because of this one church bully. Describe Diotrephes' attitude in a brief paragraph.*

3. (verse 11) *How do believers avoid that "which is evil" and follow that "which is good"?*

TRUSTWORTHY DEMETRIUS
(III John 12-14)

*O*ur third church leader is also a hero, and John urged Gaius to follow his example. Some believe Demetrius may have been John's courier, carrying this letter to Gaius, but it is impossible to know. The behavior of church members affirms or denies their claims. John encouraged Gaius (and us) to pattern our lives after the good examples.

1. (verse 12) *We understand how Demetrius could have a good reputation with other people, but how does he have "good report...of the truth itself"?*

❒ *Identify ways Demetrius is different from Diotrephes.*

2. (verse 14) *Who are the "friends" John refers to twice in this verse?*

❒ *Why would John emphasize that his readers should "Greet the friends by name"?*

DIGGING DEEPER

1. *All Bible names have a meaning. Using a Bible dictionary or encyclopedia, find the meanings of:*

Gaius

Diotrephes

Demetrius

2. *How would your congregation "handle" a domineering, malicious personality like Diotrephes?*

❏ *This book raises the issue of church discipline. Review your church's constitution and by-laws. What procedures are called for?*

3. *Apparently other believers had spoken publicly about Gaius's kind treatment (verse 6). Is there someone about whom you should offer a public affirmation?*

4. Compare II John 10-11 with III John 10. How can we know whom to receive in our homes and whom to reject?

5. In our last study, we talked about people who might profit spiritually from a letter. But in both letters John emphasizes a personal visit. List some brothers and/or sisters whose lives would be enriched by a visit from you.

<u>Who</u>   <u>Why I should visit/What I can do</u>

Now that you have your list, plan those visits.

11

Apostasy in the Church
JUDE 1–16

*I*magine this brief letter of only 25 verses using 20 words not appearing anywhere else in the New Testament. That's what we find in this critical book which addresses apostasy in the church and warns believers how to avoid it and how to deal with it.

From the text itself we know that the author was the servant of Jesus Christ and the brother of James. Scholars call this epistle "general" or "catholic" which means it was written to believers everywhere rather than a specific church such as Ephesus or Thessalonica. Some have suggested that Jude may have been writing from Israel to Assyria, Asia Minor, or even Egypt.

Jude uses a chiastic structure in which he begins and ends with the security of the believer (verses 1–2 and 24–25). Although largely judgmental (because Jude definitely wants to condemn apostasy), there is a great deal in this epistle for encouragement as well.

Jude identifies his close relationship to the Lord as a "servant." He writes with genuine humility, certainly not wanting to cause any further dissension in the church. Furthermore, he wants to avoid the unhealthy mystical significance gullible people might derive from a family connection as the Lord's half-brother.

The key verses of the epistle are 3 and 4 in which Jude states the problem and emphasizes its importance. He obviously wanted to write glowingly about their common salvation in Jesus, but, instead, was forced by the situation to urge his readers to contend for the faith.

As we study these verses, we should clearly see their application to the world in which we live where cultic heresy abounds and people who don't believe the truth are likely to believe anything.

HISTORIC JUDGMENT OF APOSTASY
(Jude 1-7)

*M*atters in this epistle are dealt with because of an urgency which the Holy Spirit laid upon the writer. When Jude discusses "the faith" in verse 3, he is not talking about personal belief but the necessity of believing and retaining true doctrine in the church.

But false teachers have already crept in, as if by a side door. They are ungodly, and they intend to exchange the grace of God with sinful behavior.

Jude begins his condemnation by recalling incidents well known to his readers, namely the example God made of Old Testament characters who fell into apostasy. Three groups come in for mention in these verses: the children of Israel (verse 5), the angels that sinned (verse 6), and Sodom and Gomorrha (verse 7). Interesting company for false teachers in the first century—and today.

1. (verse 1) *Jude doesn't refer to himself as the brother of Christ; how do we know he was?*

❒ *How do you account for the order of verbs Jude selects in this verse—sanctified, preserved, and called?*

2. (verse 3) *What is the "common salvation"?*

❒ *What deep need did Jude feel and why?*

3. (verse 4) *What does it mean that "certain men...were before of old ordained to this condemnation"?*

❒ *What does the word "lasciviousness" mean?*

❒ *Why does Jude mention the denial of both the Lord God and the Lord Jesus Christ?*

4. (verse 6) *What does it mean that God "reserved [fallen angels] in everlasting chains under darkness"?*

5. (verse 7) *In what way were Sodom and Gomorrha examples of how God deals with apostasy? What characterized their apostasy?*

CONTEMPORARY EXAMPLES OF APOSTASY (Jude 8–13)

*P*resumably the active apostates described by Jude were familiar with all the Old Testament historical references. Nevertheless, they persisted in their ways. Jude tells us they are involved in evil purposes and refuse to recognize the true authority and honor of God. As the angels rebelled against God's boundaries, as Sodom mocked moral law, as Israel refused God's leading of their nation, so these apostates refused to honor prophets, angels, or God Himself.

1. (verse 8) *Why are these men called "filthy dreamers"?*

❐ *What do the three accusatory phrases of this verse mean to you?*

• *defile the flesh—*

• despise dominion—

• speak evil of dignities—

2. (verse 9) *What is the point of this verse and what does it have to do with the body of Moses?*

3. (verse 11) *What is the "way of Cain" and what is the "error of Balaam"?*

4. (verses 12-13) *Jude uses five metaphors to describe the false teachers in these two verses; what are they?*

ANCIENT PROPHECY OF APOSTASY
(Jude 14–16)

*T*he biblical account of Enoch is found in Genesis 5. The reference to "ten thousands" merely suggests an undefinable and unlimited number of saints. Presumably, the obvious reference is to the revelation aspect of the second coming of Christ at the end of the tribulation. Several times in the book Jude reminds his readers that apostasy is nothing new since it has existed and was prophesied from ancient times.

1. (verse 14) *Describe Enoch (Genesis 5). What marks of character made him distinctive?*

2. (verses 15-16) *Why do you think Jude uses the word "ungodly" four times in one verse?*

❐ *What characterizes the ungodly?*

❐ *What is the meaning of the phrase "having men's persons in admiration because of advantage"?*

DIGGING DEEPER

1. People often use the phrase "contend for the faith" (verse 3). How can Christians do that while still maintaining a spirit of love and grace?

2. Why did the Lord deliver people He knew would not believe Him, then later destroy them (verse 5, compare Exodus 12:12, 14:1-31; Numbers 14)?

3. In your view does the phrase "strange flesh" (verse 7) mean homosexuality?

❒ Do you think this issue is a major sin today?

❒ What stance should the church take?

4. Using a Bible dictionary or encyclopedia, track down every reference to Michael the archangel. What do you learn about him?

5. *Can you think of people today who speak evil of things they don't know anything about (verse 10)? Has the Holy Spirit ever convicted you of a judgmental attitude?*

6. *Find at least two other references to the sin of murmuring and complaining in the Bible. Why do you think God calls this sin?*

 Now, consider your own record of murmuring and complaining (verse 16). If bad attitudes are a problem, will you surrender them to God as a part of your obedience to this passage?

<u>I complain about</u>   <u>Which shows this attitude</u>

❖

12

"I HOPE HE WITHSTOOD SPIRITUAL ATTACKS BETTER THAN HE DID PHYSICAL ONES."

Glorious Truth for Grievous Times
JUDE 17–25

*I*n the first century or the twenty-first, Christians will always be surrounded by doctrinal and moral error. The constant presence of sin makes it necessary to struggle daily against evil and live righteously before God.

As Jude opens this section of his letter, he emphasizes the difference between apostates and the true believers to whom he writes. The human spiritual nature in these apostates was so dominated by "soul-less" desires and forces that they were incapable of responding favorably to God's call. (Notice how frequently Jude uses triplets in this book. Verse 19 is a good example—separate, sensual, and spiritless.)

So what do believers do in this kind of environment? They must build themselves up to withstand the onslaughts around them and be pro-active in their spiritual living. Though Christians possess eternal life now, they still look to the future for immortality and glorified bodies. Until that time, Jude offers his epistle of warning but concludes it with a wonderful reminder of God's grace in the present and a genuine doxology or benediction still quoted thousands of times every Sunday morning around the world.

> *Now unto him that is able to keep you from falling, and to present you faultless before the presence of his glory with exceeding joy, to the only wise God our Saviour, be glory and majesty, dominion and power, both now and ever. Amen.* (Jude 24-25)

PERSONAL ESCAPE (Jude 17-19)

*B*y remembering the words of the Lord, believers can be warned that apostasy is real and present. How often all the New Testament writers refer their readers back to something Jesus said! Perhaps that would be a good practice in today's church as well.

1. (verse 18) *What is the connection between mocking and walking after one's ungodly lust?*

2. (verse 19) *Since these apostates do not have the Spirit, what does that tell us about them?*

❐ *In what ways might the false teachers have separated themselves from the rest of the church?*

PERSONAL EDIFICATION (Jude 20-21)

*I*n the original text, the first three words of verses 17 and 20 are identical. They show contrast with the apostates as Jude focuses on his beloved brothers and sisters in the Lord. The first thing they needed to do was to build themselves up in the holy faith, surely a reference to the body of truth God the Holy Spirit gave us in His Word.

1. **(verse 20)** *What does it mean to pray in the Holy Spirit?*

2. **(verse 21)** *How do we keep ourselves in the love of God?*

❐ *How can we look for the mercy of the Lord Jesus Christ?*

❐ *In what way will we see the mercy of Jesus Christ revealed through eternal life?*

PERSONAL EVANGELISM (Jude 22-23)

*F*ew passages in the Bible are more clear on the task of evangelism. To some people we should show compassion and for them that will be enough. Others, however, need a message of judgment, fear, and even hell fire. Jude's point seems to be that evangelism techniques must be suited to the needs of the people we are trying to reach, something recently evident in the late twentieth-century church.

1. (verse 22) *In what ways can Christians have compassion in personal evangelism?*

2. (verse 23) *What does Jude mean by the phrase "pulling them out of the fire"?*

❏ *What do you think the words "hating even the garment spotted by the flesh" mean?*

PERSONAL ENCOURAGEMENT
(Jude 24-25)

Jude does not presume that believers can accomplish all of this on their own, so he clearly shows God's part. He keeps us from falling; He will present us faultless, and for all of that He deserves our praise. In the original text, verse 25 reads, "to only God our Saviour through Jesus Christ our Lord, glory, majesty, dominion and power before all the ages and now and until all the ages. Amen." In short, God's grace will be with us to encourage us in the past, present and future.

1. (verse 24) *From what does God keep us from falling?*

❏ *How does God keep us from falling?*

❏ What does the phrase "the presence of His glory" mean?

❏ Jude also brings in the word "joy." To what exceeding joy does he refer and whose joy is it?

2. (verse 25) Does this verse refer to God the Father or God the Son?

❏ How can we give God glory and majesty?

❏ Dominion and power?

DIGGING DEEPER

1. Can you find other places in the New Testament where warnings such as those in verses 17-18 appear?

2. Many believe we live "in the last time" today. If so, we should be able to see some of the "mockers" Jude warned against. How would you describe them in modern terms?

3. *How do you practice personal edification?*

4. *Apart from organized programs at your church, in what ways do you do personal evangelism?*

5. *Jude wants to be sure his readers understand the importance of and have compassion. Name some ways you and/or your family can show compassion to lost people.*

❑ *Where can you make a difference through compassion?*

6. *Check any marginal notes or references you have in your Bible on "flesh" (verse 23). What is the "flesh"?*

❑ *How do godly people cope with fleshly problems?*

❖